Making the Best of Chromecast
Amazing Tricks and Tips

Table of Contents

Introduction

For about two years now, Chromecast has been around the scene- making it into the homes of many Americans across the country. And yet, there are so many things that many consumers don't know about this very unique and spectacular device. With 100s of apps available with Chromecast, consumers' expectations will be exceeded to the upmost, if they have the knowledge and tools available to make the best usage of this amazing product.

This book will give consumers very useful tools and tricks they can use for their fullest enjoyment possible. Their families and friends will be totally amazed, and possibly, even jealous of the fact of this extraordinary device. With this device, consumers can dismiss cable companies all together; the capability of streaming content from HBO GO, Netflix, Hulu Plus, YouTube, and other audio and video content is available; consumers can share and view different types of media and photos on TVs, tablets, laptops, and Androids simultaneously; explore YouTube parties, etc. As mentioned before, there are 100s of apps available with Chromecast. The guide that comes with Chromecast, or www.chromecast.com/apps will show all the apps that this product has to offer.

This product, which looks similar to a flash drive in appearance and size, is fully useful and powerful for a very reasonable price. With the price of $35, customers will have full usage of all of these benefits. There are other features available, such as mirroring the desktop to the TV and using a smartphone to turn on the TV.

Chromecast Setup

Before proceeding with the all the great tips and tricks for Chromecast, certain things must be downloaded if it hasn't been already. Many already have the Google Chrome Browser; however, the Google Cast extension must be downloaded as well before setting up the Google Chromecast device. Also, if Google Chrome Browser is not installed, it can be downloaded through the Chrome Web Store.

When setting up Chromecast, users should make sure that every required item is present which includes the Wi-Fi connection, a TV with an HDMI input, a tablet or smartphone, and a computer. The next thing to do is to plug the Chromecast device into the HDMI port of the TV. After that, users should visit the setup page for Chromecast on Google to download Chromecast and the required app. From there and with some details on the Chromecast package, the instructions will guide users through the fairly easy process.

One thing to note during the setting up process is some users have had problems when setting up the device. If this happens, users may have to adjust the Wi-Fi router. Also, it's important for users to visit the troubleshooting help page for Chromecast on Google.

The Breakdown of the Tips and Tricks
The following are different tips and tricks for the best utilization of this product.

1. Streaming Local Videos

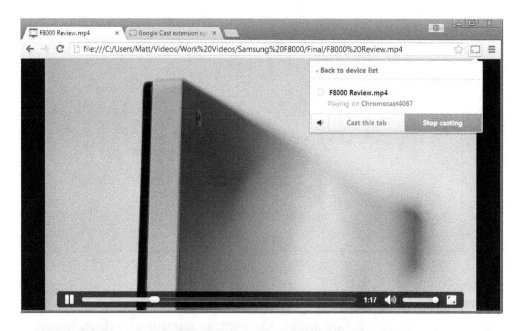

Streaming videos is possible with Chromecast. When Chrome supports a file type on a Mac or PC that have videos stored, customers can stream those videos. All that must be done, first of all, is to open the Chrome browser, and locate the desired the video. The commands to use to open the browser are CTRL and O for the PC, and Command and O for the Mac. After opening the browser, the customer must search the location where the desired video is saved. It can be on the hard drive, desktop, etc.

There are also a lot of apps that Chromecast has that can be used to play media, videos, and photos that are saved on the PC. AllCast and Localcast are some of the best apps available for the job. AllCast works with audio files, videos, and photos. Localcast may seem complicated when first launching it; however, this app is so powerful, that it has the capability to load media from different devices, such as NAS drives of the local network. It also compiles the media library of different sources automatically.

Other types of Chromecast supported apps are available as well, and the list of apps are growing as time goes on. For more information on these list of apps, it can be found on Google's website.

2. Playing any Media type using Plex

As mentioned before, there are many apps to assist with local videos; however, there are some file formats that are not supported through Google Chromecast. With that being said, that's where Plex comes in: Plex is a third party app that allow Chromecast to streamline photos, video, and audio of unsupported file formats. Plex also indexes the photos, audio, and video on the media server or computer, and it configures accordingly in order to allow Chromecast to stream photos, audio, and videos.

Once the app is downloaded, it must be led where the media is stored. From there, the app will organize all the content to be easily accessible. And with that, the customer can use a tablet, smartphone, Mac, or PC when desiring to stream with Chromecast on TV.

3. Sending websites to the TV

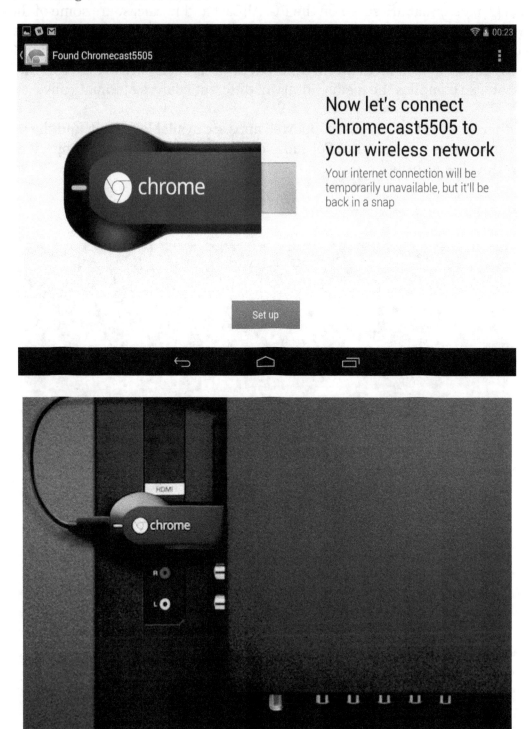

It's easy to send websites to the television from Chrome by using the Chromecast device. When viewing the desired web page for streaming, the customer must click the "Cast this tab" link in the Chromecast menu for streaming. This link is located in the right side of the address bar. This function is called casting a tab also.

4. Mirror the Android

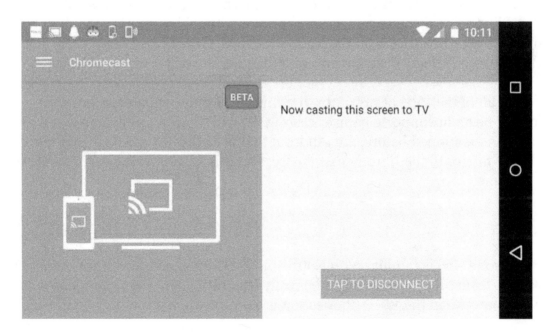

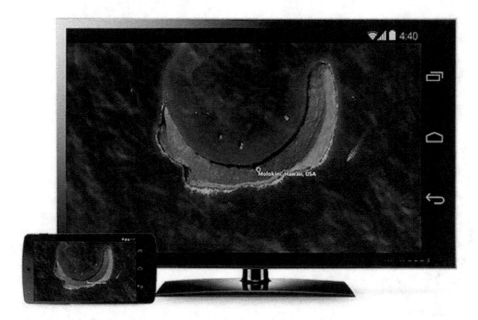

At a recent Google I/O, a new feature was introduced, and have recently became available. This new feature allows users to monitor everything on the TV through Chromecast. Most Android devices of Android OS 4.4.2 and higher have this capability, in which an Android device can be connected to the Wi-Fi network that has Chromecast.

In order to mirror the Android, certain steps must be adhered to. First of all, the Chromecast app must be opened. Then the user will select "Cast Screen", which is located underneath the navigation window. At this point, the Android is able to mirror the TV. Additionally, the user can end casting at any time, by pressing the disconnect button on the drop box that is on the Android screen. Otherwise from the Chromecast app, the user must select "Cast Screen", and then he/she will click "disconnect".

With all of the 100s of web apps, iOS, and Androids available, there will occasionally be an unsupported app of casting. So with that in mind, screen mirroring is necessary. As mentioned before, any Android that is Android 4.4.2 or higher has the capability to mirror to the Chromecast device, and this will show the exact media form on the Android.

5. Improving Video Playback by Streaming Quality Adjustment

Everyone who is familiar with Netflix or YouTube knows how buffering or lagging issues arrive from time to time. It can be really frustrating when this happens, and it usually happens when the Wi-Fi connection is slow, or when streaming traffic is high.

Chromecast, even though it works wonders when it comes to streaming, still encounter this situation on occasion as well. There are, however, a few things to do to eliminate this problem as much as possible. Therefore, to improve playback speeds, users must lower quality video by navigating the extension options in the Google Cast. Then, the "tab projection quality" must be set to "standard (480p)". When this happens, the setting's playback is set to a lower resolution.

6. Adding Emojis

Many times, users like to add a little flair to their Chromecast. One way of doing that is by adding Emojis to their Chromecast name. This could be done by going to the flower tab located in the Chromecast app for configuration. On the flower tab, the Emoji choices will populate, while the user is entering the device's name. These Emojis are also available with Mac OS X, iOS, Windows, and Android apps.

7. Hosting YouTube Parties

     Playlists are one of the notable features of Chromecast. With them, users will have the ability to set in order the desired YouTube videos to watch. And that's not all-others with different computers or mobile devices can contribute as well to the queue of YouTube, which must be on the same Wi-Fi network. Users will simply search for the video on YouTube that he/she wants to watch, add it in the playlist, and then the YouTube party is created. This works with iOS and Android devices.

8. Always Making Full Screen Videos Play

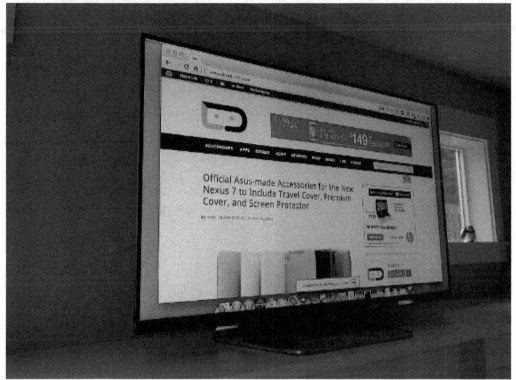

This tip applies when the video is sent from the Chrome browser on the Mac or PC. However, if something else is needed on the computer, and the user wants the streaming video from Chrome in full screen, the user must press Alt and Tab for switching tasks.

9. The Smartphone Turning the TV on

Using a remote control is ancient history for Chromecast users. Chromecast has a more unique feature that allows the TV to be turned on and switched to a HDMI input once music or videos from a tablet or smartphone is started.

Google Chromecast uses HDMI-CEC technology that is supportive by most newer brands of TVs, allowing the HDMI devices to power up those TVs. Sometimes this function is not displayed which calls for some searching throughout the TV's settings. Furthermore, the CEC function is called different things on some

17

TV brands. Some of the names for the CEC function are as follows for popular TV manufacturers: Samsung– Anynet+, Panasonic– Viera Link, Sony– Bravia Link or Bravia Sync, Toshiba– Regza Link, and LG– Simplink.

With this feature, users must plug the Chromecast first by using the AC adapter provided, as opposed to a USB port for charging. This will ensure that Chromecast is still receiving power while the television is off. While the appropriate CEC function is turned on, users must start streaming a video or music from the smartphone to Chromecast. The TV will be turned on, and the right HDMI input will be displayed for the content.

10. Using Personal Pictures as Wallpaper for Digital Photo Album Creation

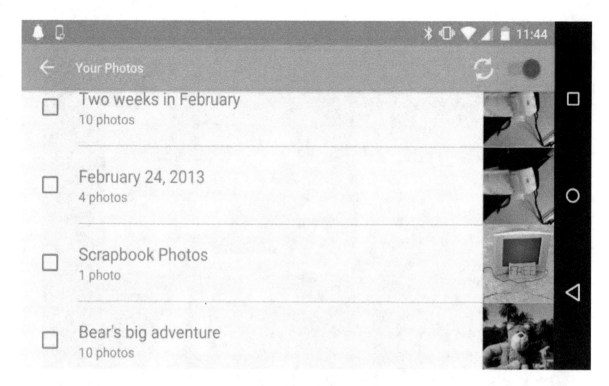

Google Chromecast has gorgeous stock photos, but users can also customize the wallpaper by having the capability through Chromecast to add photos. Google's artwork from its Cultural Institute; news outlets, such as the New York Times; satellite imagery; and weather data can also be added. However, the latest software from Chromecast and the Chromecast app on the iOS or Android device are required, even though both mobile phones should be updated automatically.

For personal photos, users must get them from a Google+ account. If Google+ isn't used often, it will be easier to make an album separately for this feature. Users would have to open the Google+ account to sign in. From there, users must click on "add photos", and drag and drop the favorites in the upload screen. Afterwards, the users will click on the "add to album", and then name the album something that is easy to remember. Once the photos are loaded, the wallpaper can be customized by opening the Chromecast app, and selecting "backdrop" that is located in the left menu. Users will then choose categories, such as "your photos", "news", "photo communities", etc.

11. Mirror the Full Desktop

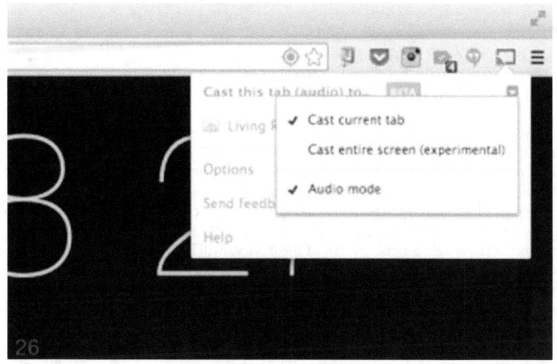

In order for the entire desktop to be sent to the TV, users must click on the drop down menu that is on the right side of the "cast this tab...." Then select the "cast entire screen". This option will require a high level of power from the computer, and video playback may be slowed down. This may also reduce video quality, and it may have a slower performance if the Mac or PC isn't very powerful. The laptop's battery will be lowered significantly as well, if not plugged. Note: The cast of the full desktop will be in experimental mode, thus causing stability issue risks also.

12. Using the Chromecast in the Hotel Room

Chromecast with portable Wi-Fi access will allow users to eliminate hotel TV for good. A portable Wi-Fi hotspot is
recommended due to the hotel's Wi-Fi having the tendency to be incredibly slow for video streaming. Also, hotels normally charge for usage on each device.

For Chromecast usage on the hotel's TV, users must first plug the device into the TV's HDMI inputs. This may not be possible with the TV being bolted to a wall or dresser, or may just be challenging. Also, most hotels don't make it easily accessible to get to the ports on the TVs. Nevertheless, once Chromecast is plugged in, users must turn the portable router on. And from there, users are required to connect the portable router to Chromecast and the mobile device, Mac, or PC, which in turn must be connected to the wireless network. All of the devices will become synced, which will allow the ability for any content to be streamed to the hotel TV, like it would be on the home TV. With this connection, users can fully enjoy the offers of Chromecast, instead of settling for the substandard hotel's Internet and cable services.

There are, though, other ways of using Chromecast in hotels. For one, some users had success by running a hotspot on the mobile phone, and then cast media directly from the laptop or phone (mobile data charges may apply). Other users have hotspot software on a laptop to get Chromecast running. Another example is when some users simply called the front desk to whitelist the device; however, mileage may vary with this method.

Some things should be noted though, when using Chromecast in hotels, and using mobile hotspots- that includes some restrictions. For one, there are data limits to mobile hotspots, and Chromecast uses data quickly. Also, some hotels restrict the usage of third party devices. So the bottom line is: It's possible to make the best usage of Chromecast in most hotels, but there may be some exceptions.

13. Factory Resetting Chromecast

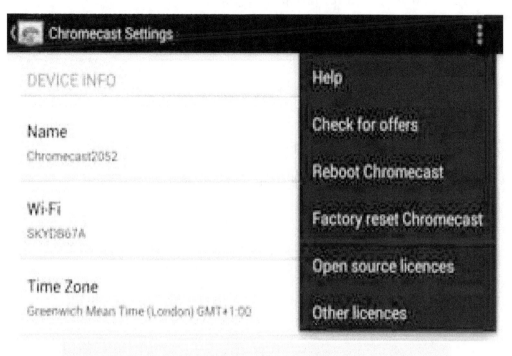

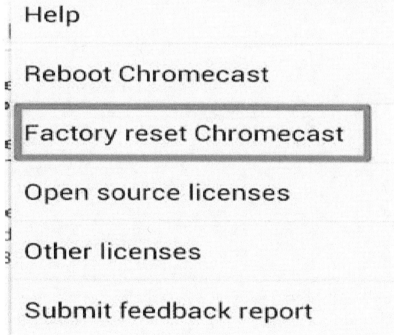

Just like computers, sometimes a technical issue can develop in which it can be resolved, and perhaps even prevent the device from functioning in its entirety. When this happens, sometimes resetting factoring settings are in order. To do this, users must access the settings menu in the Chromecast app on the mobile phone, Mac, or PC, and then select "restore factory settings". Factory settings can also be restored manually by holding down the button for Chromecast for 25 seconds.

14. Accessing the menu of Chromecast's Hidden Settings

Google Cast extension options

Changing these may have unintended consequences. Be careful.

Video Settings

Minimum bitrate: [____] kbps (min)

Maximum bitrate: [____] kbps (max)

Max quantization: [____]

Video buffer: [____] ms

Maximum tab frame rate: [____] fps

Resolution:

Audio Settings

Audio bitrate: [____] kbps (-)

Network Settings

Pacing: ☐ Enable pacing (M28 or later)

TCP: ☐ Enable audio TCP ☐ Enable video TCP

NACK: ☐ Enable Audio NACK

More Developer Settings

Some settings may not take effect until the extension is reloaded. Always reload the extension after making changes.

[Reload Extension] [Enable Log Window]

☐ Load receiver app using fling
URL for fling command:
[_____]

AppEngine receiver IDs:
[_____] add

Fixed DIAL device IPs:
[_____] [add]

☐ Enable Cloud Features

Feedback settings

☐ Enable automatic feedback after mirroring stops

For extra control over the content's streaming quality, users can access Chromecast's hidden extension options. Users must press the button for Google Cast extension, which is located on the right side of the address bar. Then the user must select "options"; right click anywhere on the page for "options"; and then click "inspect element" to get the HTML code for the page. Next, the user must expand the "quality...custom" code line, search for a few lines of text that display the words "display: none", and delete both of those lines of text. After following those steps, the Google Cast extension will appear. And while undergoing this process, it's important to keep the "options" windows open. If not, the user will have to repeat the searching and deleting of those lines that has the HTML in order to get the hidden menu again.

15. Allowing Outside Androids to Utilize Chromecast without signing to the Wi-Fi Account

Guests can send anything they want from their devices without jumping on the user's network. With the Guest mode feature, users will open the Chromecast app on the Android device. Then he/she will choose "guest mode" to slide on the feature. Then Chromecast will send an unique Wi-Fi beacon to allow other users to stream safely. This will be possible upon Chromecast's special authentication, which will further be confirmed through the inaudible audio tones.

16. Using Chromecast with Kindle Fire

Avia

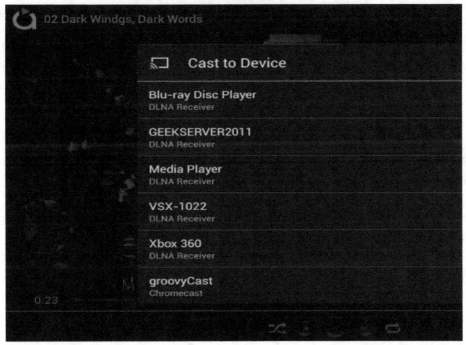

1Mobile Market

Casting is also available through Kindle Fire. Streaming apps like Pandora, Netflix, and Hulu Plus are great with the use of Kindle Fire.

With Kindle Fire HDX, it doesn't allow wireless streaming like an iPad does when it comes to music, audio, photos, and video. So since this is the case, connecting a micro-HDMI cable is required, unless users opt for third party apps. One good app in using Kindle Fire with Chromecast is called the Avia. This app allows users the capability to stream content from the Amazon's tablet to the Chromecast device. All that needs to be done with Avia is to select the cast tab that's located in the upper left side of the screen on the Kindle Fire. Afterwards, the user will select the Chromecast device for synchronization.

Another third party app is called the 1Mobilemarket Apk to use for the Kindle Fire. To get this app, users can download and install it on the Kindle. Then the users will open up this app, and search for Chromecast to play media. The next thing to do is to install each media, open the Chromecast app up, and sync the device.

This is only two apps. There are other great third party apps out there.

The ability to play games controlled by motion through the use of Chromecast and the smartphone is available. This function is not officially supported by Google, but full enjoyment with family and friends is allotted while this unique gaming approach is used with multiplayer functionality.

Google offers a game called "Super Sync Sports". This game is fairly easy to play. With this game, users must first cast the page from computer to the TV through Chromecast. The user must then follow the games instructions on the screen. And in a matter of minutes, the users and others will swing, wave, and flick the smartphone around when competing with family and friends in a virtual race. Note: It's important to keep a good grip on the smartphone to prevent accidental mishaps or injuries.

18. Launching Netflix

Netflix is one of the many apps available through Google's Chromecast. All the user has to do is to click on the Chromecast app, and proceed from there with the necessary steps and prompts in which the user will be guided to do, to launch Netflix. Once you have connected your Chromecast to your TV and Wi-Fi (wireless) network, follow the steps below to connect to Netflix. Your mobile device or computer must be connected to the same Wi-Fi network as your Chromecast. For information or assistance connecting Chromecast to your TV and/or Wi-FI network, see support.google.com/chromecast.

However, for more detailed instructions, the following steps will apply. Netflix must be launched on the iOS or Android device. It can be launched by visiting the Netflix website in the Chrome browser too.

When checking the Netflix features for Chromecast, users must select the icon for cast which is located either in the lower right side or the upper right side of the screen. Then the users must select the Chromecast device in order to launch Netflix on the TV. All that is next is to choose the TV show or movie to play.

Netflix can be controlled even more so on the TV, when deriving the Netflix app on the Nook mobile, iOS, or Android devices when synchronizing the Chromecast and the devices that the Netflix app is derived from. Transferring to another episode, pausing, rewinding, fast forwarding, etc., can be done also.

Some users have complained of still having problems with launching Netflix. If this is the case, it can be obtained if the Google Cast extension is installed in Google Chrome. Netflix can also be received directly from the computer to the TV.

19. Turning the TV into a Lava Lamp

With Chromecast, users can do so much more than to cast web pages, videos, or TV shows. This spectacular device can also display a series of video loops or pictures to set different types of moods for different types of events. TV shows, music videos and web pages aren't the only things users can cast on the TV with the Chromecast. Users can also use the Chromecast to display a series of pictures or video loops to help set the mood for any event. Revision3, for instance, provides different lava lamp videos, shots from space, crazy weather scenes, etc.

20. Using Guest Mode for Friends

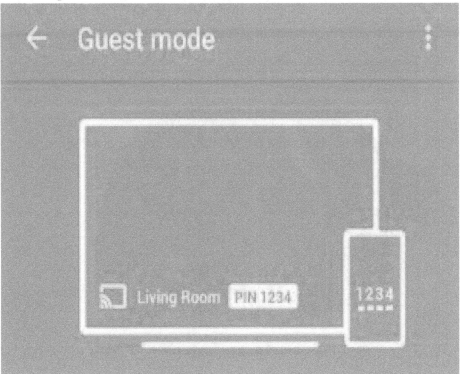

Chromecast is great to use with family and friends. Rather the user have a YouTube party with friends, by having them add videos the queue, or rather the user have relatives to use Chromecast for showing off the latest photos on a bigger screen, guest mode is the way to go. It's the way to go for this and other spectacular enjoyment and sharing among family and friends. So with that said, guests can use Chromecast without the requirement of being connected to the same Wi-Fi network.

With sounds played by the user's TV that only the user's phone can hear, this feature regarding the guest mode is made possible. As a matter of fact, there is no need to keep up with a complicated Wi-Fi password in order for guests to get started. All that must be done is to enable this process through the Android guest mode on the Chromecast app. From there, any Android nearby can cast Chromecast from different networks. Family and friends can link up to Chromecast on their devices through ultrasonic tech. However, a PIN is also available in case this fails. The PIN will be on the TV screen.

21. Using a Headphone

This is easily done by installing the earbuds into the phone to listen. Other than that, Chromecast doesn't supply a headphone for listening out of the tube. There is, however, a way for this to happen: Localcast, which is a local media app for casting, routes the audio sound to the phone as a video is played on TV. The video and audio feed must be synchronized manually, it works well after trying it out a little bit through trial and error. Localcast, however, only plays media that is saved on the phone.

22. Watching 3D VR without the Headset

Occulus Rift

Altergaze

Having the installation of the Google's cardboard app on the Android phone and a 3D TV, users can set Chromecast to the SBS mode. This mode is in the 3D settings on the TV. Then, the user must mirror the cardboard app's screen to the TV. Once that is done, the user would put on 3D glasses that came with the TV, and that's it: The user will undergo a wonderful VR experience without a VR headset.

Two wonderful 3D glasses are great choices to use in the 3D experience with Chromecast. One of them is called Oculus Rift and Alterglaze.

With Oculus Rift, this virtual reality headset is good for a great game gaming experience as players will enter virtual worlds. And of course, it's an awesome virtual experience when watching monsters reach out of the screen, and right into the living room. The Oculus Rift has custom tracking technology that allow 360 degree head tracking with really low latency. With this technology, users will feel as if they are present in the virtual world. Even the most subtle head movement is traced in real time, which creates an intuitive and natural experience. Perfect parallax, scale, and depth are created due to its stereoscopic 3D view. This device goes far and beyond the regular 3D on TV as the eyes perceive the images as if they were in the same area naturally. Also, even though the Oculus Rift looks huge to some, it's very comfortable and lightweight.

With Altergaze, these 3D glasses offer a visor with acute accuracy of stereoscopic ability. Altergaze is greatly tailored for the eyes. They come in different display sizes, a variety of focal lengths, different lens position, and different interpupillary distances. This device is so awesome that the lenses were custom made with some mathematical formulas calculated at the precise point of the center of the vision that's on the screen.

With the hardware of Altergaze, the set of lenses are interchangeable for the focal length of each smartphone display. This way, user will always enjoy the experience of the 110 FOV immersion. The optical system for Altergaze when dealing with big devices is so superior that screen resolution will not be lost, and with smaller devices, the optical system is made to magnify the image beyond the regular viewing level.

Altergaze is a hand-made crafted product, which is carefully crafted by leading partners in the field. Also, Altergaze is unique with over 8,000,000 combinations available. The product is also pre-calibrated for users.

23. Getting Free Stuff

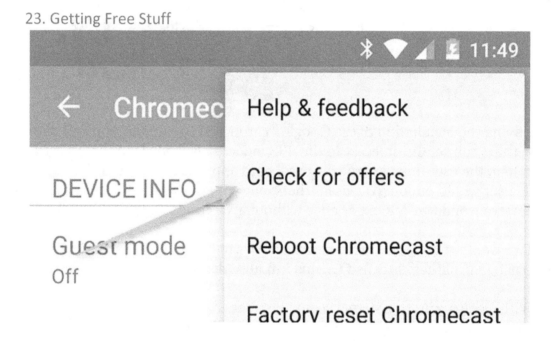

A lot of times, Chromecast is able to save its customers money. One example of this is when Google gave $20 of Google Play credit to different individuals. Google has recently gave away free copies digitally of the movie, "X-Men" (the first movie of the X-men franchise). Google also ran free promotions on services like Epix, Sesame Street Go, and Hulu Plus.

To always stay abreast of more offers that are here and to come, users must connect to the Chromecast in the iOS app or Android, and access the offers through "options". Users may also visit www.chromecast.com/offers on their computers while on their Wi-Fi network. Their Google cast extension and Chrome browser will be required.

From there, Google will search for the authentication of the device ID before relieving the information concerning offers the users qualify for. Offers are available, even if users have had Chromecast for a great while. So, it's best to check for new offers on a frequent basis.

24. Using an Audio Adaptor

Dozens of music apps are available for Android and iOS that support casting, which includes Songza, Google Play Music, Vevo, Pandora, etc. There are also a slew of radio apps and podcast players that include NPR One, BeyondPod, TuneIn, etc. Of course, all of these media forms can be cast on TV; however, with a small adapter, Chromecast can be connected directly to any stereo. Some have complained that they had problems with some adaptors, so users must search more carefully when looking for compatible brands and models.

Conclusion

For about two years now, Chromecast has been around the scene- making it into the homes of many Americans across the country. And yet, there are so many things that many consumers don't know about this very unique and spectacular device. Knowing the different tricks and tips available, along with 100s of apps available with Chromecast, users will be overjoyed with all of the knowledge and tools at their fingertips in order to get their money's worth, and then some with this amazing product. The tips and tricks for Chromecast include the following: streaming local media; playing any media type using Plex; sending websites to the TV; mirroring the mobile phone and TV; improving video playback by streaming quality adjustment; adding Emojis; hosting YouTube parties; always making full screen videos play; personalizing the wallpaper with personal photos; turning on the TV with a smartphone; using Chromecast in a hotel room; using a headphone; watching 3D VR without the headset (the Oculus Rift and Alterglaze); mirroring the full desktop; using Chromecast with Kindle Fire; resetting Chromecast back to factory settings; playing Nintendo Wii games with Chromecast and a smartphone; using outside Androids with Chromecast without being on the same Wi-Fi account; accessing Chromecast's hidden settings; turning the TV into a lava lamp; launching Netflix; using guest mode for friends; getting free stuff; and using an audio adaptor.

These useful tools and tricks will bring the fullest enjoyment possible. Families and friends will be totally amazed, and possibly, even jealous. With this device, users can dismiss cable companies all together. And furthermore, the capability of streaming content from HBO GO, Netflix, Hulu Plus, YouTube, and other audio and video content is available. The guide that comes with Chromecast, or www.chromecast.com/apps will show all the apps that this product has to offer.

Before proceeding with the all the great tips and tricks for Chromecast, certain things must be downloaded if it hasn't been already. Many already have the Google Chrome Browser; however, the Google Cast extension must be downloaded as well before setting up the Google Chromecast device. Also, if Google Chrome Browser is not installed, it can be downloaded through the Chrome Web Store.

When setting up Chromecast, users should make sure that every required item is present which includes the Wi-Fi connection, a TV with an HDMI input, a tablet or smartphone, and a computer. The next thing to do is to plug the Chromecast device into the HDMI port of the TV. After that, users should visit the setup page for Chromecast on Google to download Chromecast and the required app. From there and with some details on the Chromecast package, the instructions will guide users through the fairly easy process.

One thing to note during the setting up process is some users have had problems when setting up the device. If this happens, users may have to adjust the Wi-Fi router. Also, it's important for users to visit the troubleshooting help page for Chromecast on Google.

After all of the downloading and setting up the devices, users are ready to explore and make the best of all of their media. These steps, tricks, and tools will get users on their way to making the best of this extraordinary device. The users and their family and friends will be totally amazed of how much this tiny yet powerful device can do. Additionally, this device can be used on a plethora of platforms, such as TVs, PCs, tablets, Androids, iOS phones, etc.